21 Days

2

Greatness

By: Tyra Johnson

BK Royston Publishing LLC

Jeffersonville, IN

BK Royston Publishing
P. O. Box 4321
Jeffersonville, IN 47131
502-802-5385
http://bkroystonpublishing.com
bkroystonpublishing@gmail.com

© Copyright – 2016

Cover Design: Bill Lacy

ISBN-13: 978-0692686065

ISBN-10: 0692686061

Printed in the United States of America

DEDICATION

I dedicate this book to my Queen, my heart beat, my life, my mommy Rita McGinnis Gooden. I was there and I have seen your resilience time after time, blow after blow. Your strength that is like no other has taught me how to stand in the many adverse moments in my life. Through your example, I've learned how to choose my battles effectively and how wisdom has had to be my principle thing. Thank you for all the talks that you thought that I never heard. The wisdom that you imparted that I recognized on my journey of growth that not every little girl received from their mother. I appreciate you for loving me enough to tell me the truth over and over again. Thanks for standing strong in whom you are and for being the BEST MOMMIE a girl could ever ask for. I love you to life girl and you are my QUEEN!

ACKNOWLEDGEMENTS

First I give honor to God who has allowed me to write this book out of Holy Spirit. Thank you for believing in me Lord when no one else did. Thank you for calling me for such a time as this to empower your people into the *"Greatest You that Ever Lived."* Thank you for your image, likeness and your greatness that lies within my heart. Your anointing that allows me to Mpact the nations. Thank you for the anointing that destroys yokes, empowers, builds, and sets the captives free. I just want you to know I love you more than anything. This assignment could not have been completed without you Jesus and the amazing people you have placed in my life to love and support the endeavors that you place before me!

To my Man (husband) that happen to be my biggest supporter, pusher, lover and my friend. I love you for being an awesome husband, a spectacular father and a phenomenal

Apostle and the greatest *"PoPPoP"* on the earth. To my lovely daughters Tyrita and TyGara who are the two best INVESTMENTS I have ever invested in and the greatest young ladies a mother could ask for. Thank you both for your encouragement. Thanks for believing in your mommy. I really thank you girls for giving me sons after my own heart: Maurice and JaCorey thank you both for taking care of my girls. Thank you all for making me the proudest Abuela in the entire world. I would be amiss if I didn't thank Samaria Chever, Camryn Miller, S'kaiah Chever, Izariel (Izzy) Miller, Shyla (BOO) and my only nieto JaCorey Lamar Miller, Jr. aka (Man-Man). Thank you all for making life worth living. Abuela loves you all to life!

To my Eagles Wings Ministry of Faith family I love you all so much. Thank each of you for believing in the assignments that God has given Apostle and I. We could not do this without your support and love. EWMF is the greatest church on the Peninsula. Believe that!!!

Douglas Gooden (My Dad) thanks for loving me. Tomaja Johnson thanks for the prophetic dream, here is the book and the pens. Sharon Johnson thank you for seeding into my dream. I thank Regina Turner for believing in me in BIG ways I could never thank you enough girl for your love towards me. I thank you and Karen Wilkins for every seed sown, every reprimand, every call and every beat down that got us here. I thank you ladies from the bottom of my heart.

Last, but definitely not least my Life Coach Master D. (Dawniel Winningham) girl you have blessed my life beyond spoken or written words. I am so honored to know you and to have been a part of Passion Changers 2016. So much has been pulled out of me since then. Thank you for loving me enough to push me into the *"Greatest Tyra that has ever lived!"*

INTRODUCTION

"Let him who would move the world first move himself."

-Socrates-

How do we move from the mundane to the miraculous? This is a question that I've asked for years. This statement hung on a banner on the back wall of our church in 2000 as our yearly theme. It caused me to say to God, "there has to be more to you Lord than what I'm giving. How do I move from this day-to-day run of the mill life? How do I tap into the amazing, extraordinary you that I see so many others walking in." Then, I said to God "if you didn't come to avenge, punish nor inflict us, how do I get to the salvation that reflects your power, your authority and your greatness? How do you rescue, restore and ensure salvation in my life? How do I learn to conqueror, overpower and prevail?"

This book may challenge some of your traditional thoughts about your greatness. It might make you say hmmm when it comes to who you were created to be. I encourage you to INHALE and allow God to fill those greater places within your heart, mind and soul. Open up to the greater abilities, accomplishments, the greater king and the greater God that lays dormant in the crevices of your desire to be and to move from the mundane to the miraculous.

No doubt there is an abundant fierceness and greatness that exist, accompany and remain within you. A strong desire that you feel that you must DO. A distinct demonstration that defines your greater from all others. Moving according to your God consciousness by the negotiating wars and experiences that hinder you from "Mobilizing in your Greatness."

I come with the anointing from my Father to not only challenge you, but to unleash your desire to live BIG in CHRIST. To dream mega and to cause you to impact the world with the greater that is within. As Socrates quote stated, if we are going to move the world it must first start within. It is imperative that we begin with those uneventful, unexcited mind sets, actions and thoughts. Remember, the assignments that God gave you, He entrusted into your heart? Recall the request you've desired that has never manifested, they are still there come on lets transform our minds and lets go higher and higher in the Lord. Let's move, conqueror, and achieve because there is someone out there who is awaiting your greatness for Greater is He that is in you than he that is in the world.

I

Believe In Your Greatness

Ephesians 3:20
*"Now unto Him that is able to do exceeding abundantly
above all that we ask or think, according to the power that
worketh in us."*

Knowing that the ability to "Do" and exercise in your

greatness comes with an abundance that is more than you

could request, believe, understand or apprehend. If you

continually display your greatness, if you repeatedly

operate out of your God consciousness it reveals an

unspoken manifestation of God's brightness that becomes

operative without end. Execution in the belief of your

greatness puts a demand on His glory expanding a place for

God to pour out His exceeding abundance above all into the

work of the Power that is at work in you.

Affirmation:

I operate in Greatness.

II

Envision Your Greatness

Habakkuk 2:3
"For the vision is yet for an appointed time; but at the end it shall speak, and not lie; though it tarry, wait for it; because it will surely come, it will not tarry."

The appointed time of your vision shall send out a clarion call that is flawless. It may linger, but the promise is that if you envision it, recognize it, anticipate its arrival and if you look for your dreams, they have been set up by God to not only show up at its proper, fixed time, but they must advance you. Your visual greatness is unavoidable. Though it may linger it is not worthless. Delay never means denied! Dominate in your abundance and watch it be fulfilled.

Affirmation:

I don't only see my Greatness, but I Pursue it with a

Vengeance!

_____

_____

_____

_____

_____

_____

_____

_____

_____

_____

_____

_____

_____

_____

_____

_____

_____

III

Intentional Greatness

Jeremiah 29:11
"For I know the plans I have for you" declares the Lord
"Plans to prosper you and not to harm you, plans to give
you a hope and a future."

God's created plan for your life releases the reliable

character that allows you to prosper deeply in the quality of

your ability to be great.

The expectancy of God carries a deliberate, calculated

consciousness of intentionality that creates provision and

purpose within you that allows your greatness to be

intentional enough 2 manifest your Destiny.

Affirmation:

I Prosper in the Intentional Plans of God with intensity &
Purpose 2 meet Destiny!

_____

_____

_____

_____

_____

_____

_____

_____

_____

_____

_____

_____

_____

_____

_____

_____

_____

_____

IV

Kingdom Greatness

Matthews 6:33
*"Seek ye first the Kingdom of God, and His righteousness;
and all these things shall be added unto you."*

Greatness is birthed out of your desire to be in the right place at the right time. It is determined by your deliberate, intentional plans to be in order, on time and important in your Kingdom equity of character to demonstrate God's visible presence.

It is Show Time and it's your Kiros moment to reveal God's divinity of His royalty, rule and His realm. It's time to show God's emperor abilities of kingly distinctions that lies within your heart as a believer. Seeking God First gives you chief aim of not only added righteousness but His divine authorship of the volume of the book that has been written of you!

Affirmation:

I Seek God's demonstration of deliberate, intentional and imperial divine increase!

_____

_____

_____

_____

_____

_____

_____

_____

_____

_____

_____

_____

_____

_____

_____

_____

_____

_____

_____

_____

V

Meditating Greatness

Psalms 111:2
*"Great are the works of the Lord; they are pondered by all
who delight in them."*

The making of your fabric, threads the desired essence of

the BIGGER that requires the soaking, meditation and

delight of the Lord which pushes you to achieve out of your

place of worship. Worship produces our miracles and

prompts you to accept there is purpose in each moment

spent with God. So, I summons you to Soak your way into

giving birth to your Phenomenon!

Affirmation:

My phenomenon shows up in the essence of my worship!

_____

_____

_____

_____

_____

_____

_____

_____

_____

_____

_____

_____

_____

_____

_____

_____

_____

_____

VI

Praying In The Now

Hebrews 11:1
"Now faith is the substance of things hoped for the evidence of things not seen."

The significance of your greatness will begin in your ability to pray in the "Now." It's right now faith that moves your substance into your hopes of fulfilling the greatness you were created for. The quality of your vision, the essence of your perceptions will catapult you into the confidence of the distinction of your character that reveals the mega, abundance of the Divine, deliberate greatness that lies within you.

It is now, being without limited confidence and assurance we have in Jesus that promotes us into the solidified weight of His glory that pulls out the ability of the BIG commitments of our actions of hope, motive and plan that originates through our capacity to declare and produce our NOW!

Affirmation:

I am persuaded in the proof of my unaware realities of my NOW!

_____

_____

_____

_____

_____

_____

_____

_____

_____

_____

_____

_____

_____

_____

_____

_____

_____

_____

_____

VII

Prevailing Purpose

Proverbs 19:21
"Many are the plans in a person's heart, but it is the Lords purpose that Prevail."

There may be many devises in your heart. Many things that you desire to accomplish. Great designs, skillful plots, celebrated inventions, undivided thoughts and determined ways, but it is YHVH, ELOHIM's advice, council, designs, intentions, aspirations and advancements that shall arise. His plans for your life shall be established. The persuasion of Christ's conquering purposes shall be created and instituted and exemplified in your Triumphant You! It is His accomplishments in your plans that will advance you into the Greatest you that Ever Lived.

Affirmation:

I am Triumphant in Gods Prevailing Plans for my Greatness!

_____

_____

_____

_____

_____

_____

_____

_____

_____

_____

_____

_____

_____

_____

_____

_____

_____

_____

_____

_____

VIII

Think BIG

Proverbs 23:7(a)
"For as a man thinketh in his heart so he is!"

The appetite of your greatness should calculate you into the Ruach breath of your sum thoughts that causes you to apprehend your Greatness. Allowing you to devour and consume freely God's mighty power that lies within the stomach of your soul.

Affirmation:

The expression of the intensity of my appetite produces my Greatness!

_____

_____

_____

_____

_____

_____

_____

_____

_____

_____

_____

_____

_____

_____

_____

_____

_____

_____

IX

Evaluate Ur Greatness

II Corinthians 13:5
"Examine yourselves to see whether you are in the faith, test yourselves. Do you not realize that Christ Jesus is in you—unless, of course, you fail the test?"

Realizing that your faith, confidence, assurance and trust in your Greatness that God has placed in you is to mobilize accordingly to His heart beat. Examine your genuine ability to become great. Making sure that the source, belief and fidelity is all persuaded by the birthing of your desire to yield to God. Test yourself continually for counterfeit substances, bogus character and imitating qualities that could pull you away from the true U. Evaluating your greatness is seen as the Real Deal anything aside from that would be counterfeit.

Affirmation:

I mobilize in my Greatness from an authentic place of Faith!

_____

_____

_____

_____

_____

_____

_____

_____

_____

_____

_____

_____

_____

_____

_____

_____

_____

_____

X

Positioning for Perfection

Philippians 3:12
*"Not that I have already obtained all this, or have already
arrived at my goal, but I press on to take hold of that for
which Christ Jesus took hold of me."*

Paul said I don't mean to say that I have already achieved,

fulfilled or perfected these things. But I press. I am

practicing, pursuing and positioning myself to possess. You

may not have obtained, accepted nor experienced all the

greatness that lies within you. Your goals may not appear

near to accomplish, but don't give up the pursuit. Keep

shadowing that you may not only embark upon it but you

may seize and possess your distinct character and your

strong weight. Continue to posture yourself to fulfill and

accomplish the orientation of the prominence that you have

been stationed to receive. The same way that God arrested

and understood the assignment that He created you for is

the same way you catch, hold tight and fulfill your

greatness.

Affirmation:

The arrest of God has positioned me to fulfill & to lay hold of God's Plan for my Life!

_____

_____

_____

_____

_____

_____

_____

_____

_____

_____

_____

_____

_____

_____

_____

XI

Crave Ur Greatness

Psalms 37:4
"Delight yourself also in the Lord and He shall give you the desires of your heart."

Delicately handling the brilliance and quality of the Lord will cause God to yield, provide and perform accordingly to the petitions of your understanding of the way you take delight in Him. Requesting your visual desires and imagination of your Greatness will open up your space to receive the deep things within that will permeate you into being the best you that ever lived.

Affirmation:

I Crave the brilliance of the quality of the Lord that utters forth the petitions of my bravest me!

_____

_____

_____

_____

_____

_____

_____

_____

_____

_____

_____

_____

_____

_____

_____

_____

_____

_____

_____

XII

Reigning out of a Place of Rejection into the Greatest U.

Romans 8:1
"Therefore there is now no condemnation for those who are in Christ Jesus, who walk not after the flesh, but after the Spirit."

It is imperative as you reign out of your rejected place into your now, you understand there are facts that precede your present case. Your right now time, your worthless punishments, penalties and verdict to your conditions, welfare and experiences hold no validity to where you are going in the Spirit. When you are in your undisturbed place, when the ditch deserted moments are no longer a part of your behavior, when your impetuosity has been given a right to occupy your day-to-day life. The dominating power within begins to conduct itself excessively in the movement of the wind, breath and Spirit placing the authority of the anointed one Jesus Christ to reign. Pushing out abandonment and rejections allowing

you to reign in your ability to influence and walk in your

Greatness.

Affirmation:

I am free from all condemnation, conditions & rejections I

walk in the influencing Power of Christ Jesus that created

the Greatest me that has ever Lived!

_____

_____

_____

_____

_____

_____

_____

_____

_____

_____

_____

_____

XIII
Manufacturing Your Miracles

Deuteronomy 10:21
"He is your praise, and he is thy God, that hath done for thee these great and terrible things, which thine eyes have seen."

He is your praise (Tahilla) song, quality, deeds, depths, your deep place and He is your God Elohim; the divine representative of divine majesty and power that performs, accomplishes, advances and appoints your greatness. Yahweh causes you to be astounded and in awe of what you have already seen and accessed, experienced, understood and displayed within your own eyes, confidence, wish and sight.

It is the quality of your song, the standard of your actions, the character of your depths and the value of your deep place that Elohim's divine presentation and manufacturing miracles of power is performed, accomplished and advanced. It is your greatest abilities of your fearful reverence of His majesty that causes astonishment and awe of His Super-Natural Power that you have seen explained, understood and manufactured with what you have not only seen, but glared at, wished for and had confidence to manufacture and walk in the greatness of your miracles.

Affirmation:

I Perform, Accomplish & Advance in my greatest ability of Yahweh's Super Natural Power that manufactures the greatness of my Divine Miracles!

XIV

Work the Work of Your Greatness

John 9:4
"I must work the works of Him that sent me, while it is day: the night cometh, when no man can work."

It is inevitable that you perform and minister about the great actions of the one that dispatched, permitted and granted you without limits at sunrise to sunset. When night arrives no one and nothing will have the capability, strength or power to minister about the greatness that at night becomes useless to perform within your proficiency. So, it behooves us and it's necessary for us to commit to the deeds that have been transmitted in our greatness and do it before it disappears! Because whatever you don't use, you lose and your greatness is too BIG to be unsecured!

Affirmation:

I work limitless in my Strength supplying security to all that has been granted unto me from sunrise to sunset apprehending my Greatness!

_____

_____

_____

_____

_____

_____

_____

_____

_____

_____

_____

_____

_____

_____

_____

_____

_____

_____

XV

Exposing Your Expectations

I Corinthians 9:10(b)
*"This is written: that he that ploweth should plow in hope;
and that he thresheth in hope should be partakers of his
hope."*

In uncovering the expectancy of your greatness you must

embrace your confidence to mobilize toward the certainty

of your faith that you are able to take part, share, & belong

in the greatness of your hope, faith & trust that *has already*

been composed, written & released in your Greatest U!

Affirmation:

*I participate in the Hope of my calling of the Greatest me
that ever Lived!*

_____

_____

_____

_____

_____

_____

_____

_____

_____

_____

_____

_____

_____

_____

_____

_____

_____

_____

—————————⟡—————————

XVI

Building on Veracity

John 16:13
"Howbeit when he, the Spirit of truth, is come, he will guide you into all truth: for he shall not speak of himself; but whatever he shall hear, that shall he speak: and he will show you things to come."

The veracity of your greatness can only be located by the

Spirit of truth. It will lead, instruct and teach you the value

of the strength that lies in the crevices of your character.

Truth proceeds into the portals of your consciousness

releasing the fullness of your never ending impressed

proclamations Jesus declared, announced and reported that

would arrive out of His ability to form and create you in

His likeness.

Show up in your Now!   Show up in your Truth!   Show up

in your Greatness!

Affirmation:

I show up in my Now! I show up in my Truth! I show up in my Greatness!

_____

_____

_____

_____

_____

_____

_____

_____

_____

_____

_____

_____

_____

_____

_____

_____

_____

_____

_____

XVII

Perceived Power

Mathews 22:23
"The eye is the lamp of the body. If your eyes are healthy, your whole body will be full of light. But if your eyes are unhealthy, your whole body will be full of darkness. If then the light within you is darkness. How great is that darkness."

The potential lamp that releases the direction of your greatest turns, and movement will always be envisioned out of the index, shape and vigor of your mind. This powerful faculty of knowing originated out of influences of your ideas, belief and convictions that brings clarity of the sound brilliance and transparency of your divine life in Christ Jesus! I produce results that shine and make manifest the manifold wisdom of God of my greatest capabilities. I dare you to start blowing up out of your healthy place of surveying power. The power of accomplishments that sets you on a lamp stand that all may see the quality of your

Creator. The more you understand, the more you believe,

the greater you become in Christ.

Affirmation:

I mobilize & influence out of a space of brilliance. Shining the power of wisdom from the quality, understanding & belief to become greater in Christ!

_____

_____

_____

_____

_____

_____

_____

_____

_____

_____

_____

_____

_____

_____

_____

_____

_____

XVIII

Intimacy

Exodus 31:3
*"And I have filled him with the Spirit of God, in wisdom,
and in understanding, and in knowledge, and in all manner
of workmanship."*

The quality of your greatness permeates you to your full

strength, courage and mind that will thrust you into the

intimate place with Elohim's great and divine ability which

presents the wisdom to recognize good from bad, left to

right and up and down. The Ruach of God teaches you how

to discern the process of construction that reveals the

affinity of your ability as you perform out of your place of

functionality of His wind, breath and thoughts. The

creativity of Elohim's wisdom, understanding and

knowledge is enough intimacy to unleash the workmanship

of the greatness that will turn your dreams into realities.

Affirmation:

In to me God sees & breathes His Ruach that produces my workmanship of greatness!

_____

_____

_____

_____

_____

_____

_____

_____

_____

_____

_____

_____

_____

_____

_____

_____

_____

_____

XIX

My Weakest Strength

Isaiah 40:29
"He gives power to the weak, and to those who have no might He increases strength."

In the creativity of your workmanship God provides the supply of power that gives you the ability and multiplicity that increases your greatness. Strength that forces your weaknesses, your spiritual fatigues of your mind and spirit to push out of its unfathomable, unsearchable, powerless levels to the vigor, maturity and wealth that exceeds and brings forth the abundance you were created for.

Affirmation:

The power to multiply in the maturity of my abundance is supplied by God!

_____

_____

_____

_____

_____

_____

_____

_____

_____

_____

_____

_____

_____

_____

_____

_____

_____

_____

_____

XX

Workable Love

"You can see God from anywhere, if your mind is set to love and obey Him." -A.W. Tozer

Your dreams, visions and greatness can only be achieved out of your place of love, for the Bible declares if you love me you will keep my commandments. Obedience is imperative in how we are capable of apprehending and visualizing your greatest love that will birth your sight to see and obey in a place of workable love! See it, love it, work it and achieve it! This is your greatest work!

Affirmation:

I navigate, see, love, work & achieve my greatest work in loving & obeying my God!

_____

_____

_____

_____

_____

_____

_____

_____

_____

_____

_____

_____

_____

_____

_____

_____

_____

_____

_____

_____

_____

XXI

Suddenly

Isaiah 48:3(b)

"My mouth announced them and I make them known; then suddenly I acted, and they came to pass."

The mind releases a sound of evidence that explains and describes the greatest proclamation of obedience that places an advancement on your mobilizing greatness which produces solidity, character, strength and quality, *Suddenly* and *Immediately* that causes you to rise and shine in your arrival.

Affirmation:

The declarations of my mouth establishes the now Faith that acts in my Suddenly!

_____

_____

_____

_____

_____

_____

_____

_____

_____

_____

_____

_____

_____

_____

_____

_____

_____

_____

_____

_____

XXII

Resurrected Resilience

Galatians 6:9
"Let us not be weary in well doing: for in due season we shall reap, if we faint not."

In greatness one can't afford to be driven by negative influences, experiences of weariness nor fainting. The resilience of the excellence that God has manufactured in you comes to a head propelling you to advance in the proper time. Allowing you to collect in your season of "DO" that encourages those around the appealing greatness to be inspired, revived and resuscitated by the elasticity of the work, acts, and the GREATNESS of GOD!

Affirmation:

The resilience of the Excellency of God resuscitates my DO season of Greatness!

_____

_____

_____

_____

_____

_____

_____

_____

_____

_____

_____

_____

_____

_____

_____

_____

_____

_____

_____

Daily Affirmations:

1. *I operate in Greatness.*

2. *I don't only see my Greatness, but I Pursue it with a Vengeance!*

3. *I Prosper in the Intentional Plans of God with intensity & Purpose 2 meet Destiny!*

4. *I Seek God's demonstration of deliberate, intentional, imperial divine increase!*

5. *My phenomenon shows up in the essence of my worship!*

6. *I am persuaded in the proof of my unaware realities of my NOW!*

7. *I am Triumphant in Gods Prevailing Plans for my Greatness!*

8. *The expression of the intensity of my appetite produces my Greatness!*

9. *I mobilize in my Greatness from an authentic place of Faith!*

10. *The arrest of God has Positioned me to Fulfill & to lay hold of God's Plan for my Life!*

11. *I Crave the brilliance of the quality of the Lord that utters forth the petitions of my bravest me!*

12. *I am free from all condemnation, conditions & rejections I walk in the influencing Power of Christ Jesus that created the Greatest me that has ever Lived!*

13. *I Perform, Accomplish & Advance in my greatest ability of Yahweh's Super Natural Power that manufactures the greatness of my Divine Miracles!*

14. *I work limitless in my Strength supplying security to all that has been granted unto me from sunrise to sunset apprehending my Greatness!*

15. *I participate in the Hope of my calling of the Greatest me that ever Lived!*

16. *I show up in my Now! I show up in my Truth! I show up in my Greatness!*

17. *I mobilize & influence out of a space of brilliance. Shining the power of wisdom from the quality, understanding & belief to become greater in Christ!*

18. *In to me God sees & breathes His Ruach that produces my workmanship of greatness!*

19. *The power to multiply in the maturity of my abundance is supplied by God!*

20. *I navigate, see, love, work & achieve my greatest work in loving & obeying my God!*

21.   *The declarations of my mouth establishes the now Faith that acts in my Suddenly!*

Bonus: *The resilience of the Excellency of God resuscitates my DO season of Greatness!*

About the Author

"A Kingdom Voice -- Mpacting U to Greatness"

Ambassador Tyra Johnson better known as AmbaTj is the Co-Founder of Eagles Wings Ministry of Faith. She is a trailblazer with several five-fold ministry gifts, an author, a certified life empowerment specialist, dynamic speaker, teacher and motivator. Her passion is Prophetic Intercession that specializes in equipping warriors for the advancement of the Kingdom. She is best known as a life strategist and respected prophetic intercessor that can transform, translate, convert and revolutionize people for the Kingdom of God.

As a prophet of God, she has given her life to hearing and heeding the voice of God which enables her to coach, activate, permeate, and equip End-time Prophetic Intercessors to declare and decree the Word of God that are assured with confidence in the declaration until it is established.

In 2002, she received her ministerial license at Bibleway Evangelistic Church International, Okinawa, Japan. In 2003, she obtained a degree in ministry from Vision University, and received her certification in Chrisian Counseling from the American Association of Christian Counseling. In 2008, she thoroughly enjoyed studying at Kingdom University under the mentorship of Dr. Cindy Trimm. Tyra is a Board Certified Advance Life Coach Specialist who specializes in Developmental Empowerment for women. In 2014, "The Paga Xperience" a prophetic empowerment/prayer movement that is affecting thousands worldwide was birthed. In January 2016, AmbaTj branded herself and launched a Six Week empowerment course, Mpact Dreamers 2016; fulfilling her passion to Mpact and empower women to "Become the Greatest You that ever Lived."

Ambassador Tyra relishes that God has given her the opportunity to assist her husband Apostle Garcia Johnson in ministry. She believes her first assignment is to be a queen to her king and raise her two beautiful daughter's to be queens in their own homes. In that great allotment, she has received two sons, five amazing grand-daughter's and her only grandson.

Tyra delights herself in the LORD and prides herself in exemplifying agape love to those that God places in her realm of influence. She abides on the fact that what she makes happen for others, God will make happen for her. She is on a effectuate journey to arise, define vision, take counsel and go after WISDOM for it is better than gold.

www.ingramcontent.com/pod-product-compliance
Lightning Source LLC
Chambersburg PA
CBHW060428090426
42734CB00011B/2489